DOLLHOUSE PEOPLE

DOLLHOUSE PEOPLE

VIKING KESTREL

A Doll Family You Can Make

BY TRACEY CAMPBELL PEARSON

*I want to thank Regina Hayes and Barbara Hennessy for
all their help and their unending patience in making
this book, and a special thank you to Erin Whelan,
Suzanne Pool, and Lisa Leffingwell.*

VIKING KESTREL
Viking Penguin Inc., 40 West 23rd Street, New York, New York 10010, U.S.A.
Penguin Books Ltd, Harmondsworth, Middlesex, England
Penguin Books Australia Ltd, Ringwood, Victoria, Australia
Penguin Books Canada Limited, 2801 John Street, Markham, Ontario, Canada L3R 1B4
Penguin Books (N.Z.) Ltd, 182-190 Wairau Road, Auckland 10, New Zealand

First edition
Copyright © 1984 by Tracey Campbell Pearson
All rights reserved
First published in 1984 in simultaneous hardcover and paperback editions
by Viking Penguin Inc.   Published simultaneously in Canada
Printed in U.S.A.
1 2 3 4 5 88 87 86 85 84

Library of Congress Cataloging in Publication Data
Pearson, Tracey Campbell.   Dollhouse people.
Summary: Includes patterns and easy-to-follow instructions
for making the various members of the Littlefield doll family.
Accompanying text relates the family's history from the first meeting of the
grandparents to the arrival of all the Littlefield grandchildren.
1. Dollmaking—Juvenile literature. [1. Dollmaking. 2. Dolls. 3. Handicraft] I. Title.
TT175.P43 1984   745.592'21   83-25992   ISBN 0-670-43433-7

CONTENTS

This book is about a family, the Littlefield family. You will meet Charles and Sarah Littlefield, their children Elizabeth, Jonathan, and Lucy—the new baby—Grandmother and Grandfather Littlefield and, of course, Mr. Buff and Bumkins, the dog and cat. You will learn how they became a family and then you can sew your own tiny family.

Your family dolls can be plain or fancy. They can live in a beautiful dollhouse, on a shelf, or even in your pockets. You can sew one very special family or an entire town of families.

Before you begin to sew, read through a few chapters. Next, choose the doll you would like to sew first. Then you will be ready to begin.

CHAPTER ONE

Before You Begin

The Littlefields weren't always a big little family living in a big little house like this one.

It all began quite a long time ago, at a potluck supper. Grandfather tasted Grandmother's blueberry pie. He said it was so wonderful, he would marry the girl who baked that pie.

Grandmother's mother took him at his word. Soon they were married, and after a while a very important event took place: Charles was born.

Dollhouse People

Where to Begin?

At home! Start by collecting things. Show the list below to your family and friends and see if they can help you.

Do you know people who sew? Ask them if they will save fabric scraps for you. It doesn't take much fabric to make a tiny dress. You can even use fabric from old clothes. (Just check with Mom or Dad first.) Lightweight fabrics like cottons are perfect. Think small. Look for tiny prints, little dots, skinny stripes, little checks, and pretty solids.

If you know some people who knit, have them save their leftover yarn. You can use yarn for hair or you can try using frayed rope or string, or cotton, for Grandma and Grandpa.

Collect trims and ribbons, fat and skinny, plain and fancy. Look at the list for ideas. You could put your collection in plastic bags, so you can see what you have while you're working on a doll: one bag for fabric scraps, one for hair, one for trims, and a little box for buttons, hooks, and beads.

With bags of goodies in front of you, you can feel free to experiment while you sew.

look at my collection!!

wow!

4

Before You Begin

Things to Collect

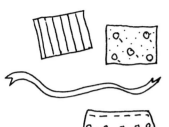 Fabric *(cotton is best, tiny prints, patterns, and solids)*

 Ribbons and trims *(rickrack)*

Lace

Thread *(different colors)*

 Yarn *(different colors and textures, for hair)*

 String, rope, cotton *(for hair)*

 Skinny wire *(for glasses)*

 Tiny hooks and snaps

 Tiny buttons

Little beads *(for buttons or necklaces)*

Basic Supplies

Here are some basic supplies you will need:

Sewing scissors (the most important supply for sewing, handle them with care. They should *never* be used on paper—that will make them dull.)

Scissors for paper

Needles

Straight pins

Pencil

Paper (thin, for tracing clothing patterns. You can buy tracing paper; thin typing paper also works.)

Ruler

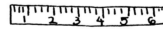

Tweezers (helpful for turning little things right side out)

Iron

Dollhouse People

Basic Stitches

Sewing is easy. It just takes practice. Before you make a doll, make sure you understand these simple stitches. If you have never sewn, ask a parent or someone who sews to help you.

Practice on fabric scraps. Draw a seam line on the fabric with a pencil and try to follow it. First try straight seams, then try curved ones. When your stitches are even and stay on the seam line, then you are ready to sew.

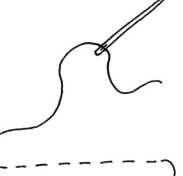

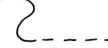

RUNNING STITCH

This is the easiest stitch. It is used to hem the dolls' clothes or for sewing seams.

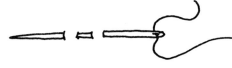

Insert the needle through both layers of fabric, bring it back out $\frac{1}{8}$ inch ($\frac{1}{2}$ cm) farther along your stitching line.

Insert the needle $\frac{1}{8}$ inch ($\frac{1}{2}$ cm) farther along your stitching line, bring it back out $\frac{1}{8}$ inch ($\frac{1}{2}$ cm) farther along your stitching line.

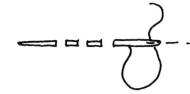

Repeat this in and out pattern, following your stitching line.

Try to keep your stitches and your spaces equal in length.

Before You Begin

BACKSTITCH

This is a basic stitch used for sewing the dolls and their clothes. Think of the backstitch as taking two steps forward and one step backward. Do this stitch two times at the beginning and end of each seam and it will keep your seam from coming undone.

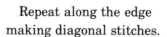
double backstitch

Insert the needle through both layers of fabric, bring it back out $\frac{1}{8}$ inch ($\frac{1}{2}$ cm) farther along your stitching line.

Put the needle in again where you started and pull it out $\frac{1}{8}$ inch ($\frac{1}{2}$ cm) farther along the stitching line.

Continue to follow the stitching line in this manner.

Remember to end your seam with a double backstitch.

OVERCASTING STITCH

This stitch is used to sew the dolls' legs to their bodies.

Insert the needle through both layers of fabric. Bring the needle back up and over the edge of the fabric.

Repeat along the edge making diagonal stitches.

Dollhouse People

GATHERING

Gathering is a way of sewing a bigger piece of fabric to a smaller one. It is easy to do, and once you know how to gather, you can add ruffles to a simple dress and make it very special.

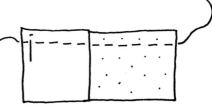

To practice cut two pieces of fabric scraps, a square and a rectangle.

Draw a seam line ¼ inch (¾ cm) from the long edge of the rectangle, and another on the square.

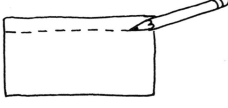

Following your seam line on the rectangle, make a row of running stitches. Do *not* secure each end of your seam with a double backstitch or a knot. Instead, leave about 3 inches (8 cm) of extra thread on each end.

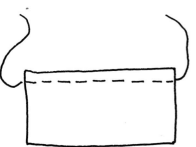

With the right sides together, matching the seam lines, pin the square to the rectangle where the edges meet.

You are ready to gather! At the pinned end, hold the extra thread (you can wrap the thread around your finger). Pull the thread at the other end of the rectangle, until the fabric puckers up and becomes the same length as the square.

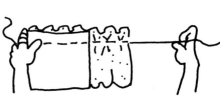

Even out your gathering so that it isn't all lumped in one place and pin the gathered fabric to the flat fabric.

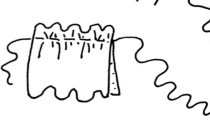

Using the backstitch, sew the gathered fabric to the flat fabric, following your seam line.

When you are finished, take out your pins and remove the extra piece of thread.

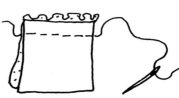

Before You Begin

Paper Patterns

All of the patterns in this book are traceable! Sometimes, you will be able to trace the patterns directly onto your fabric, as explained in Chapter Two. But, often you will be using fabric in colors and prints. With the following instructions you can trace paper patterns.

Once you have made the patterns, label and save them. They can be used again and again to make a whole wardrobe. Two dresses from the same pattern can look entirely different, if you just change the fabric and trims!

MAKING PATTERNS

1. Using a sheet of paper thin enough to see through, place the paper over the pattern you have chosen.

2. With a pencil, trace the pattern onto the paper. Trace everything on the pattern, and label it.

3. Cut out the paper pattern along the cutting line, using your paper scissors.

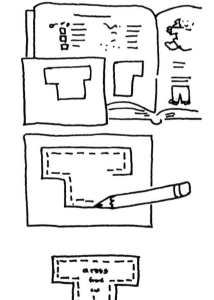

_____
cutting line

- - - - - -
sewing line

TO CUT THE PATTERN OUT OF FABRIC

1. If the pattern is marked "cut 1," pin the paper pattern to the right side of one piece of fabric.

2. Cut the fabric, cutting as close to the pattern edge as you can, without cutting the paper.

3. When the pattern is marked "cut 2," put the paper pattern on top of two pieces of fabric, with the WRONG sides together. Pin the pattern to BOTH layers of fabric. Cut through both layers of fabric at the same time.

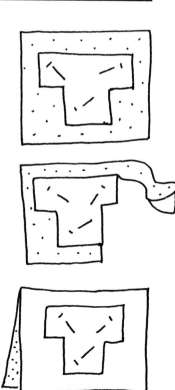

Dollhouse People

Helpful Hints

The more you sew, the easier it becomes. Here are some helpful hints that will make sewing even simpler for you.

KNOW YOUR FABRIC

There are lots of different types of fabrics! I have recommended cotton for the dolls and their clothes because it is lightweight and easy to work with. When you have more experience with sewing you may want to try other fabrics. With scraps of felt or wool you can make winter pants for the family. Sweaters made from old socks will keep off the winter chill.

RIGHT SIDE VS. WRONG SIDE

The color is usually stronger on the right side of the fabric, more faded on the wrong side. If your fabric is "solid," all one color, or both sides look the same—then don't worry about it.

For the illustrations in the book, the right side will be shown with dots; the wrong side will be blank.

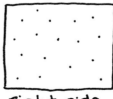

right side   wrong side

Before You Begin

GLUE

Glue can be very helpful when you are sewing tiny things. If your fabric begins to fray from too much handling, dab some white glue, or even clear nail polish, on the edge to stop the fraying.

Instead of sewing on buttons and trims, some people find it easier to use glue. You can also use glue to help hold the hair in place on your dolls.

When you are working with white glue, put a little puddle of glue onto a piece of paper. Use a toothpick to apply it to small places. If it is too thick, use a little water to thin it down.

PRESSING

Irons are hot! Ask a parent for help *before* you use one or press without one. Just place a piece of paper over the seam you want to press and rub hard with your fingernail or a spoon.

FINALLY

The most important hint of all is to take your time. Take each project one step at a time. Don't try to make an entire family in one sitting. Choose one doll, one piece of clothing, and before you know it you will have an entire family with so many clothes, they won't be able to decide what to wear!

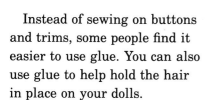

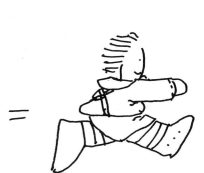

CHAPTER TWO

Making the Dolls

It was quite a few years later, at another potluck supper, that Charles met Sarah.

This time it was Charles's pie that received all the attention. He told Sarah the recipe was a family secret.

Charles promised to share the recipe, but only if Sarah promised to marry him.

The Littlefield family was growing larger!

Dollhouse People

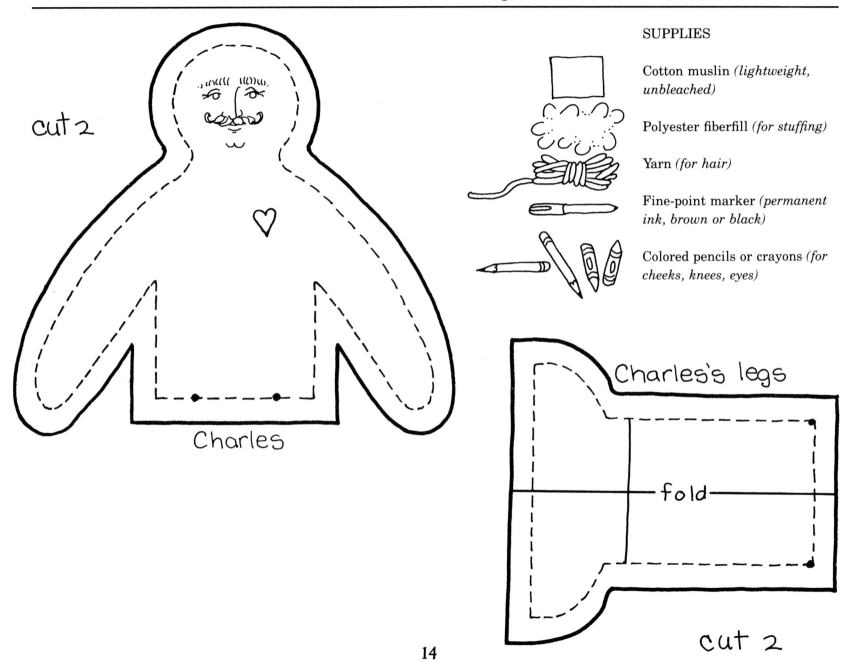

cut 2

Charles

SUPPLIES

Cotton muslin *(lightweight, unbleached)*

Polyester fiberfill *(for stuffing)*

Yarn *(for hair)*

Fine-point marker *(permanent ink, brown or black)*

Colored pencils or crayons *(for cheeks, knees, eyes)*

Charles's legs

fold

cut 2

14

Making the Dolls

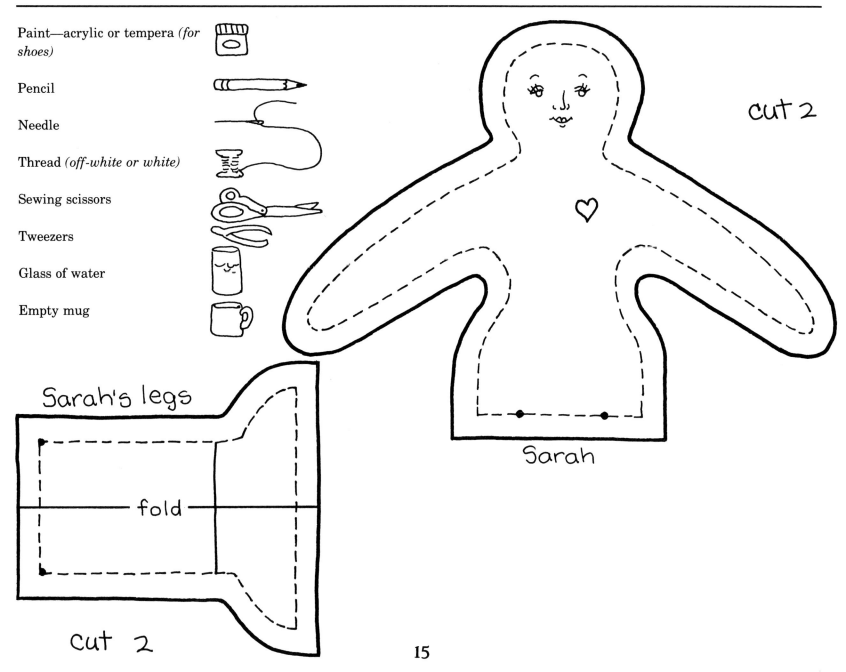

Paint—acrylic or tempera *(for shoes)*

Pencil

Needle

Thread *(off-white or white)*

Sewing scissors

Tweezers

Glass of water

Empty mug

cut 2

Sarah

Sarah's legs

fold

cut 2

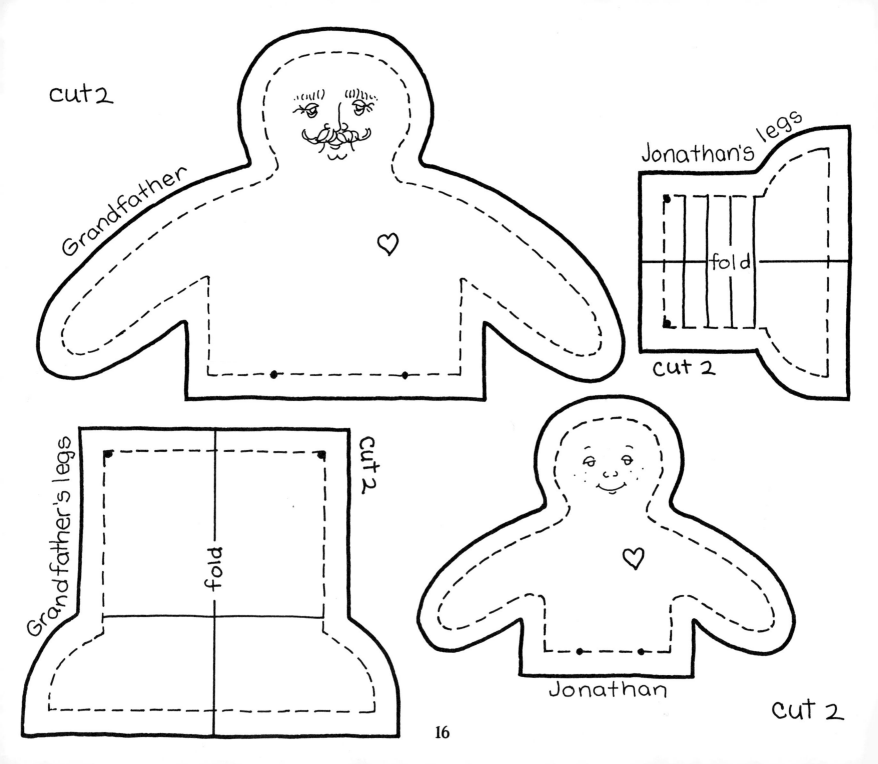

cut 2

Grandfather

Jonathan's legs

fold

cut 2

Grandfather's legs

cut 2

fold

Jonathan

cut 2

16

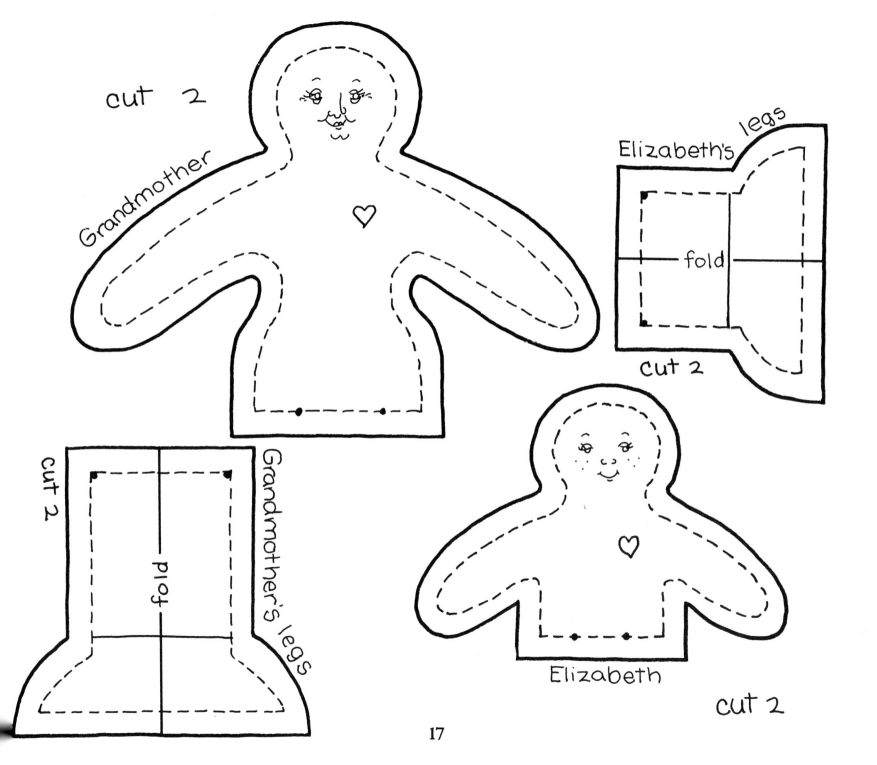

cut 2

Grandmother

Elizabeth's legs

fold

cut 2

cut 2

fold

Grandmother's legs

Elizabeth

cut 2

17

Dollhouse People

Sewing the Dolls

First choose the doll you want to make. Before you begin to sew, read through all the instructions.

If you plan to use the doll faces that are in this book, practice tracing them, with your pen, on scraps of muslin first. Otherwise, make up your own faces.

CUTTING OUT THE PATTERN

1. Cut out two squares of muslin fabric, 7 inches (17½ cm) for adult dolls, 5 inches (12½ cm) for the children.

2. Place on square of fabric over the pattern for the upper body of the doll you have chosen.

3. If you are copying the doll face from the book, read this; otherwise go on to 4. Trace the doll's face right onto the muslin, using the marker. When you are done, turn the fabric over and place it back over the pattern in the book, face down this time.

4. With a pencil trace the pattern onto the muslin square—tracing first the seam line ▬ ▬ ▬, then the cutting line ▬▬▬ .

PINNING

1. Place the other muslin square under the one you just traced (your seam lines facing up).

Making the Dolls

2. Pin the squares together, placing the pins inside the doll's body.

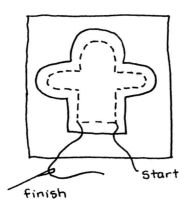

SEWING THE UPPER BODY

1. Using the backstitch, sew around the body. Begin at the bottom, follow the seam line, but remember to leave the bottom open for stuffing.

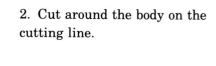

Start

finish

2. Cut around the body on the cutting line.

clip

3. Clip where it is shown on the pattern. Be careful not to clip into your seam.

4. Turn the body right side out—first the head, then the arms. You may need help with the arms. This is where the tweezers are helpful. Use them to pull the arms through. Be gentle; you don't want to rip the fabric. Ask a parent for help if you need it.

STUFFING

Stuff the body with fiberfill. First the head, then the arms, and finally the belly. Use a pencil or toothpick to smooth the stuffing into tight places.

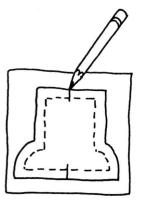

THE LEGS

1. Cut two pieces of muslin, each 4 inches (10 cm) square.

2. Place one square over the leg pattern and trace it as you did for the upper body. Mark the fold lines.

Dollhouse People

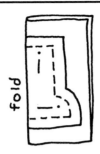

PINNING

1. Fold the leg in half along the fold lines (lengthwise), with your drawing on the outside.

2. Pin inside the seam line.

STUFFING THE LEG WITHOUT PIPE CLEANER

Stuff the leg with fiberfill, beginning at the toe and filling the leg.

Now repeat for the other leg.

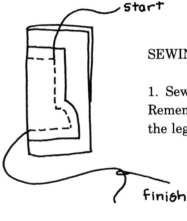

SEWING THE LEG

1. Sew along the seam line. Remember to leave the top of the leg open for stuffing.

2. Trim, by cutting along the cutting line. Clip as shown on the pattern.

3. Turn right side out.

FINALLY

TO ATTACH THE LEGS TO THE BODY

1. Insert one leg ¼ inch (¾ cm) into the upper body. Make sure the foot is facing forward. Match the dot on the body front to the seam on the leg.

2. Pin the leg in place, beginning at the dot and working your way around the outside of the leg.

3. Repeat with the other leg.

4. If there is a space in between the legs, pin it closed.

Making the Dolls

TO SEW

Sew the legs to the upper body, using the overcast stitch. Begin at the front of one leg, follow the seam line around the outside of the leg. Continue across the lower body, closing

any opening as you sew. Keep sewing around the other leg. Finish at your starting point.

Now you are ready to sew on the hair.

Hairstyles

Here are some ideas for hairstyles. You can try these or make up your own. The instructions call for sewing the hair to the head, but you can use glue instead if you prefer.

CUTTING YARN

A simple way to cut yarn for hair is to wrap the yarn around a piece of cardboard, a postcard, or even a small book. Wrap the yarn around the cardboard several times. Cut the yarn at one end of the cardboard. This will give you several strands of yarn the same length.

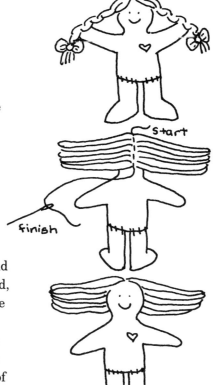

ELIZABETH'S HAIR

1. Cut a few strands of yarn about 8 inches (20 cm) long.

2. Center the yarn on the back of Elizabeth's head. Cover the back of the head to the seam at the top of her head. Pin.

3. With a double backstitch, sew the yarn to the head, following a straight line to make a part. Begin at the center of the top of the head and finish at the center back of the head.

Dollhouse People

Now you can decide how you want Elizabeth to wear her hair. She can let it hang and wear it long, or cut it and wear it short. She can wear a ponytail, pigtails, or braids. Elizabeth can even wear braids pinned to the top of her head.

SARAH'S HAIR

1. Cut a few strands of yarn about 8 inches (20 cm) long.

2. Center the yarn on the back of Sarah's head. Pin.

3. Twist the yarn on one side of Sarah's head, bringing the yarn to the top of her head, covering the seam line. Pin at the center of the top of the head. (Do not worry about the excess yarn yet.)

4. Repeat for the other side.

5. Twist the remaining excess yarn together into a bun on the back of the head. Pin.

6. Sew the hair to the doll's head.

GRANDMOTHER'S HAIR

Follow the instructions for Sarah's hair. Try using cotton or fiberfill for Grandmother's hair.

JONATHAN'S HAIR

Using a few strands of yarn about 3 inches (7½ cm) long, follow the instructions for Elizabeth's hair.

After sewing the part, sew the yarn in place along the sides of the head.

Trim the excess yarn.

CHARLES'S HAIR

1. Cut a few strands of yarn about 4 inches (10 cm) long.

2. Center the yarn on the back of Charles's head. Turn under the edges of the yarn at the seam on the doll's head. Pin.

3. Sew the yarn in place.

Making the Dolls

Try sewing on eyebrows. Cut a tiny piece of yarn for each eyebrow and sew the eyebrows to the head.

GRANDFATHER'S HAIR

Follow the instructions for Charles's hair. Try using cotton or fiberfill. You can add a mustache or even a beard.

Coloring

This is where you give the family a healthy glow. Use a red- or pink-colored pencil or crayon and practice on a scrap of muslin. Then color the cheeks, knees, and heart on your doll. Try using a color for the eyes.

You can even color striped stockings on Jonathan's legs, as they are in the book.

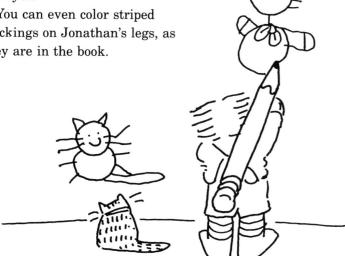

Painting

The family's shoes are painted on. Using a small brush and acrylic or tempera paint, first try painting on a scrap of muslin before you paint on a doll.

When you are ready, paint the shoes on the doll. Be careful not to get paint on the rest of the doll.

To dry the shoes, put your doll headfirst in a mug or glass so the feet are sticking up.

If you want to add buttons to the shoes, you can do so when the shoes are dry. Just add dots of white paint on the outside of the shoes.

Finally, while you are waiting for the paint to dry, wash out your brush.

CHAPTER THREE
Charles & Sarah

When Charles and Sarah were first married, they lived on a shelf. Sarah took great care in decorating their first home. Charles agreed that it was quite cozy.

Every afternoon Sarah would make tea, and Charles and she would sit together and plan their future. They had wonderful plans!

Dollhouse People

Sarah's Clothing

SUPPLIES

Basic Supplies *(introductory chapter)*

White cotton fabric *(for pantaloons and blouse)*

Tiny calico-print cotton fabric *(for skirt)*

Ribbon *(for skirt, about 14 inches long, $1/2$ inch wide [35 cm long, $1^{1}/_{2}$ cm wide])*

Assorted pieces of lace and ribbon *(for blouse and pantaloons)*

Tiny beads or buttons *(for blouse)*

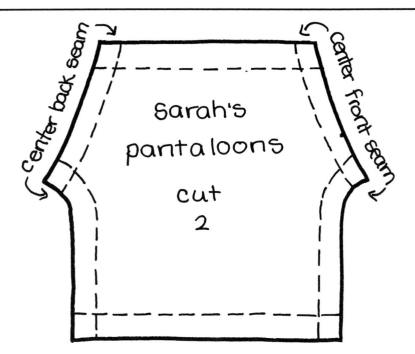

center back seam

center front seam

Sarah's pantaloons cut 2

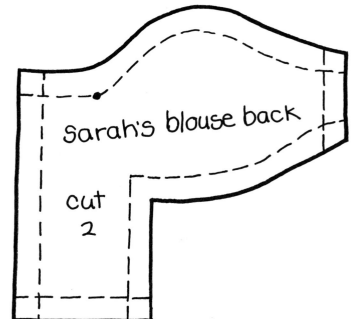

Sarah's blouse back cut 2

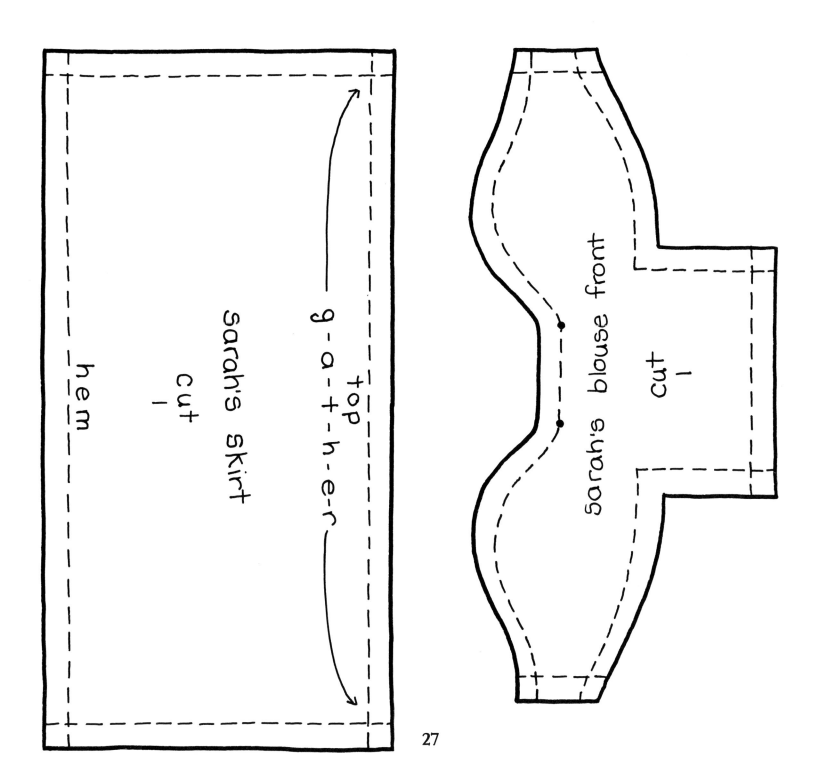

hem

Sarah's skirt

cut
1

top
g-a-t-h-e-r

Sarah's blouse front

cut
1

27

Dollhouse People

Sarah's Pantaloons

Sarah's pantaloons are like pants with lace!

First use the pantaloon pattern to cut your fabric, as explained in Chapter One.

TO SEW THE PANTALOONS TOGETHER

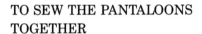

1. With right sides together, match the center front seams. Pin.

2. Begin at the top of the pantaloons, sew, following the center front seam to the inner leg.

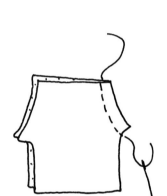

TO HEM PANTALOONS

1. Turn under the waist $\frac{1}{4}$ inch ($\frac{3}{4}$ cm). Press.

2. Hem using the running stitch.

3. Turn under the pantaloon legs $\frac{1}{4}$ inch ($\frac{3}{4}$ cm). Press.

4. Hem using the running stitch.

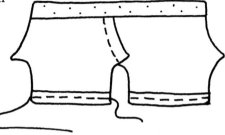

TO ADD LACE OR TRIM

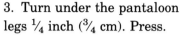

1. Cut the trim to fit the pantaloon legs.

2. Pin the trim to the right side of the legs.

3. Sew the trim in place using the running stitch.

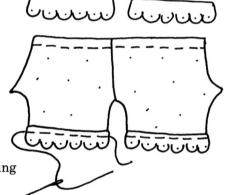

TO FINISH SEWING PANTALOONS TOGETHER

1. With right sides together, match the center back seam. Pin.

2. Begin at the top of the pants, sew, following the center back seam to the inner leg.

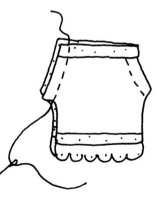

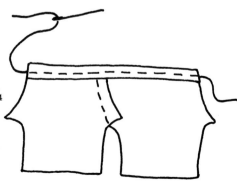

Charles & Sarah

3. Now turn the pantaloons so that the two legs are facing front. With right sides together, match the inside leg seams. Pin.

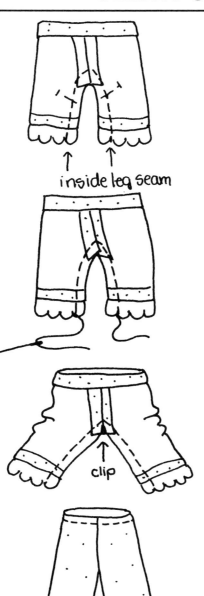

inside leg seam

4. Begin at the bottom of one pantaloon leg, sew, following the inside leg seam up the leg, turn the corner and continue back down the other leg.

5. Clip as shown.

clip

6. Turn pantaloons right side out.

Sarah's Skirt

Sarah's skirt is simple to make! Be sure to read about gathering before you begin!

First use the skirt pattern to cut your fabric, as explained in Chapter One.

SKIRT HEM

1. Turn under the bottom edge of the skirt $\frac{1}{4}$ inch ($\frac{3}{4}$ cm). Press.

2. Hem using the running stitch.

TO GATHER

Gather the top of the skirt to 4 inches (10 cm) in length, as explained in Chapter One.

TO ATTACH SKIRT TO RIBBON

1. Cut a ribbon about 14 inches (35 cm) long.

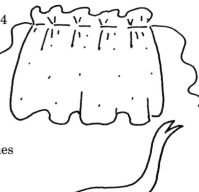

Dollhouse People

2. With the right side of your gathered material and the right side of the ribbon facing out, center and pin the ribbon onto the skirt, making sure to cover the raw gathered edge.

3. Pin the skirt to the ribbon.

4. Sew the skirt to the ribbon.

FINALLY

1. With right sides together, match center back seam. Pin.

2. Begin at the bottom edge of the skirt and sew, following the seam to the dot.

3. Turn the skirt right side out.

TO ADD A RUFFLE

Before you begin the skirt:

1. Cut ¾ inch (2 cm) off the bottom of the skirt pattern.

2. Cut a strip of fabric 1½ inches (4 cm) wide and 12 inches (30 cm) long.

3. Wrong sides together, fold the strip of fabric in half lengthwise. Press.

4. Gather the strip (both layers) ¼ inch (¾ cm) from the raw edges, until it equals the width of the skirt bottom.

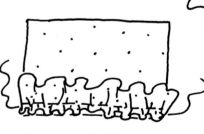

5. Do NOT hem the skirt! Instead, match the ruffle edges to the right side of the skirt edge. Pin the ruffle in place.

6. With a ¼ inch (¾ cm) seam, sew the ruffle to the skirt bottom. Press the seams toward the top of the skirt.

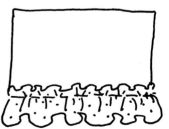

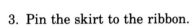

Charles & Sarah

7. Go back to page 29, and continue skirt with "to gather." There is no need to hem the skirt. You did that while you were making the ruffle!

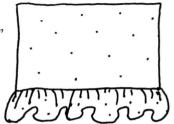

Sarah's Blouse

Sarah's blouse is a fancy T shape. Sew the basic blouse, then add lace and trim to make it special.

First use the blouse pattern to cut your fabric, as explained in Chapter One.

TO SEW FRONT TO BACK

1. With right sides together, matching seams, pin the front of the blouse to the back at the shoulder seams.

2. Begin at the end of one sleeve, sew, following the seam line to the little dot.

3. Repeat for other sleeve.

TO HEM SLEEVES

1. Turn under the sleeve bottoms ¼ inch (¾ cm). Press.

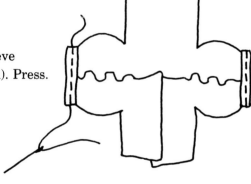

2. Hem using the running stitch.

(To add lace to sleeves see page 45.)

TO SEW SIDE SEAMS

1. With right sides together, matching seams, pin the front of the blouse to the back.

Dollhouse People

2. Begining at the sleeve bottom, sew, following the sleeve seam. Turn the corner and continue following the side seam to the bottom of the blouse.

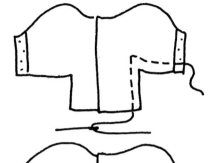

3. Repeat for other side.

4. Clip as shown.

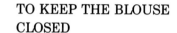

TO HEM BLOUSE

1. Turn under the bottom edge of the blouse ¼ inch (¾ cm). Press.

2. Hem.

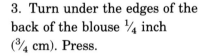
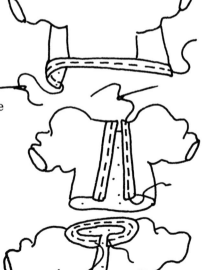

3. Turn under the edges of the back of the blouse ¼ inch (¾ cm). Press.

4. Hem.

5. Turn under the neck of the blouse ¼ inch (¾ cm). Press.

6. Hem.

FINALLY

Turn the blouse right side out.

TO KEEP THE BLOUSE CLOSED

1. Sew a snap or hook to the back of the blouse.

2. Sew a narrow ribbon to the neck of the blouse.

TO MAKE YOUR BLOUSE SPECIAL

1. Add lace or ribbon to the collar or cuffs, or lace to the front and back of the blouse.

2. Add buttons or beads to the front and back of the blouse.

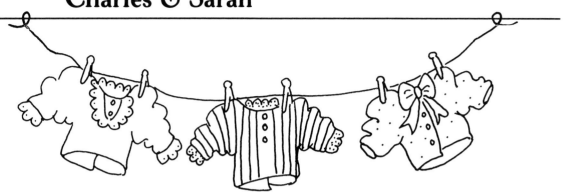

3. Use a tiny checkered or striped fabric, or a pretty print.

4. Add a ruffled collar (see Sarah's nightgown).

Charles's Clothing

SUPPLIES

Basic supplies *(introductory chapter)*

White cotton fabric *(for shirt)*

Cotton fabric *(for pants)*

Skinny ribbon for suspenders *(for pants)*

Tiny beads or buttons *(for coat and shirt)*

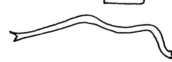

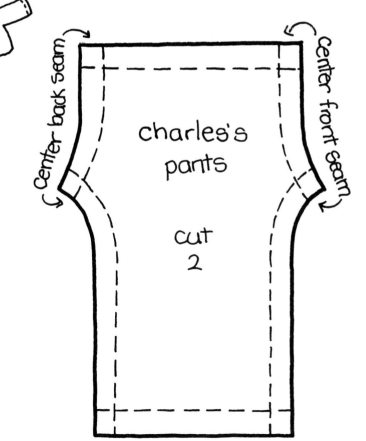

Center back seam

Center front seam

charles's pants

cut 2

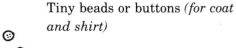

Dollhouse People

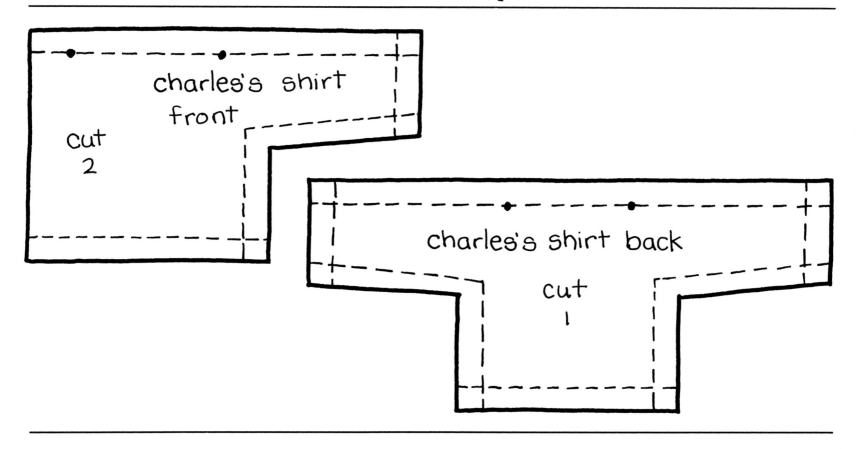

charles's shirt
front

cut
2

charles's shirt back

cut
1

Charles's Pants

Charles's pants are like pantaloons without lace. Use these same instructions for Jonathan's and Grandpa's pants too.

First, use the pants pattern to cut your fabric, as explained in Chapter One.

TO SEW THE PANTS TOGETHER

1. With right sides together, match the center front seams. Pin.

2. Begin at the top of the pants and sew, following the center front seam to the inner leg.

TO HEM WAIST AND LEGS

1. Turn under the waist ¼ inch (¾ cm). Press.

2. Hem using the running stitch.

3. Turn under the pant legs ¼ inch (¾ cm). Press.

4. Hem using the running stitch.

TO FINISH SEWING PANTS TOGETHER

1. With right sides together, match the center back seam. Pin.

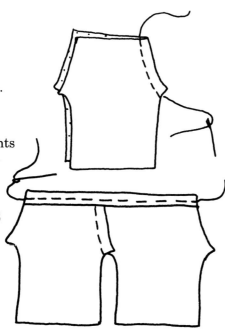

2. Begin at the top of the pants and sew, following the center back seam to the inner leg.

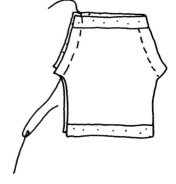

3. Turn the pants so the two legs are facing front. With right sides together, match the inside leg seams. Pin.

4. Begin at the bottom of one pant leg and sew, following the inside leg seam up the leg, turn the corner and continue back down the other leg.

5. Clip as shown.

6. Turn right side out.

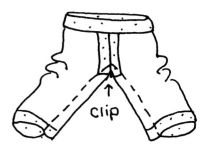

clip

Dollhouse People

FINALLY
THE STRAPS

1. Cut two pieces of narrow ribbon 4 inches (10 cm) in length (3½ inches [9 cm] for Jonathan, 4½ inches [11 cm] for Grandpa).

2. Place the ribbons ½ inch (1½ cm) inside the front of the pants. Pin.

3. Sew the ribbon in place.

4. Cross the ribbon, careful not to twist it, and place the ribbon ½ inch (1½ cm) inside the back of the pants. Pin.

5. Sew the ribbon in place.

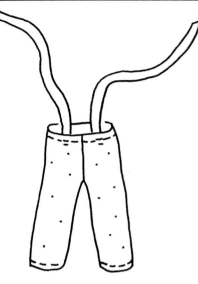

TO MAKE YOUR PANTS SPECIAL

1. Use a checkered or striped fabric to make dress-up pants!

2. Add pockets!

3. Add cuffs to the pants!

TO MAKE PANTS WITH CUFFS

Start by making the pant leg pattern ½ inch (1½ cm) longer. Follow the instructions for sewing the pants, only hem the pants with a larger hem, about ½ inch (1½ cm). When you've finished sewing the pants, turn up the hems ¼ inch (¾ cm) to form the cuffs.

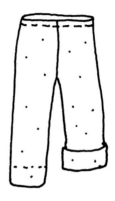

Charles's Shirt

First, use the patterns for the shirt to cut your fabric, as explained in Chapter One.

FRONT FOLDS

1. With right sides together, fold one side of the shirt front along the centerfold line, matching dots. Pin.

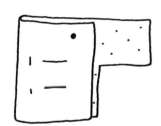

2. Begin at the dot and sew, following the seam line, along the top of the shirt to the edge of the fold.

3. Repeat along the bottom edge.

4. Turn the shirt front right side out. Press flat.

5. Repeat for other side.

TO SEW FRONT TO BACK

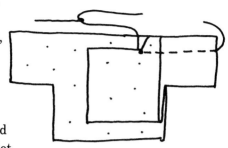

1. With right sides together, match dots and arm seams of one side of the front of the shirt to the back. Pin.

2. Begin at end of sleeve and sew, following seam to the dot.

3. Repeat for other side.

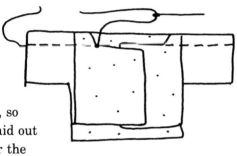

4. Press the seams open, so that the whole shirt is laid out flat, with the opening for the head in the middle.

TO HEM SLEEVES

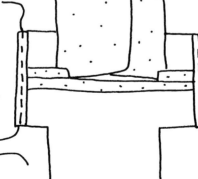

1. Turn under the sleeve bottoms ¼ inch (¾ cm). Press.

2. Sew using the running stitch.

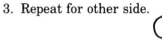
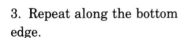
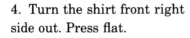

Dollhouse People

TO SEW SIDE SEAMS

1. With right sides together, match the side and sleeve seams. Pin the front of the shirt to the back.

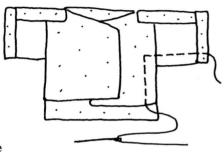

2. Begin at the edge of the sleeve and sew, following the seam line along the edge of the sleeve, turn the corner and continue down the side of the shirt to the bottom.

3. Repeat for the other side.

4. Clip as shown.

clip   clip

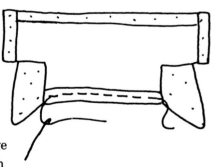

FINALLY

1. Turn under the bottom edge of the back of the shirt ¼ inch (¾ cm). Press.

2. Sew using the running stitch.

3. Turn under the back neck ¼ inch (¾ cm). Press.

4. Sew using the running stitch.

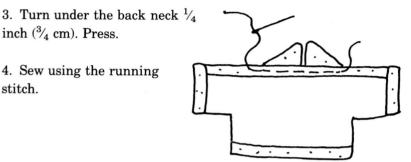

5. Turn right side out.

6. Sew tiny beads or buttons to the front of the shirt.

7. To keep the shirt closed, use a piece of yarn, ribbon, or embroidery thread. Just tie it around the neck of the shirt after Charles puts it on!

Charles & Sarah

TO MAKE YOUR SHIRT
SPECIAL

1. Use cotton fabrics in
different colors and patterns.

2. Add a tiny pocket.
Use this pattern to make a
little pocket and you can put
one anywhere. Turn under all
of the edges of the pocket $\frac{1}{4}$
inch ($\frac{3}{4}$ cm) and press. Pin the
pocket to the front of the shirt
and sew it in place using the
running stitch. If you leave the
top of the pocket open you can
put things in it.

3. Make cuffs.

Read "To Make Pants with
Cuffs." Remember to think
shirt sleeves instead of pant
legs, arms instead of legs!

pocket pattern

I like pockets!

so does froggie!

CHAPTER FOUR

Elizabeth & Jonathan

After Elizabeth and Jonathan were born, it became clear that the young family had outgrown their tiny home.

The children were very active, and Sarah was afraid they might fall off the shelf and hurt themselves. Luckily, Charles found a wonderful house with lots of room for the children to play in.

Jonathan especially liked the porch.

Dollhouse People

Elizabeth's Clothing

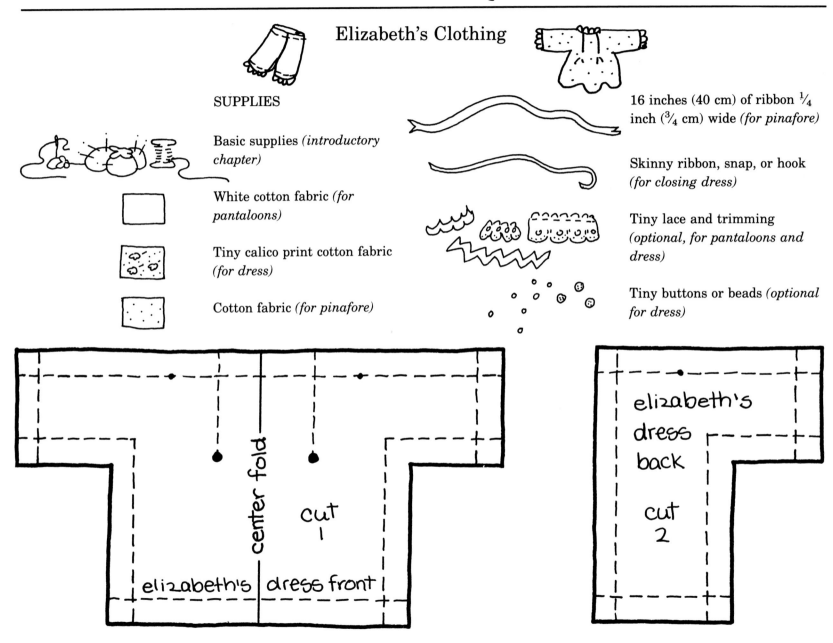

SUPPLIES

Basic supplies (*introductory chapter*)

White cotton fabric (*for pantaloons*)

Tiny calico print cotton fabric (*for dress*)

Cotton fabric (*for pinafore*)

16 inches (40 cm) of ribbon ¼ inch (¾ cm) wide (*for pinafore*)

Skinny ribbon, snap, or hook (*for closing dress*)

Tiny lace and trimming (*optional, for pantaloons and dress*)

Tiny buttons or beads (*optional for dress*)

center fold

cut 1

elizabeth's dress front

elizabeth's dress back

cut 2

Elizabeth & Jonathan

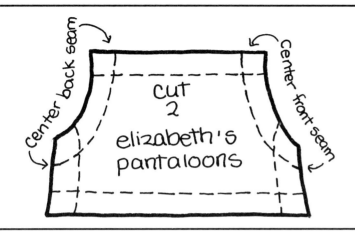

cut 2 elizabeth's pantaloons

center back seam

center front seam

Elizabeth's Pantaloons

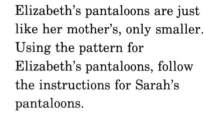

Elizabeth's pantaloons are just like her mother's, only smaller. Using the pattern for Elizabeth's pantaloons, follow the instructions for Sarah's pantaloons.

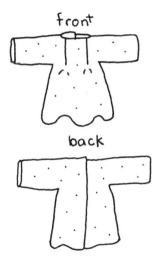

front

back

start

finish

Elizabeth's Dress

Elizabeth's dress is a T shape with a tuck in the front. Start with the basic dress, then add trimmings and buttons.

First, use the dress pattern to cut your fabric, as explained in Chapter One.

DRESS FRONT

1. With wrong sides together, fold the dress front in half along the centerfold line, matching the tuck seams. Pin.

2. Begin at the top of the dress and sew, following the seam line to the little dot.

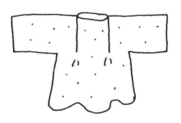

3. Press the panel flat.

TO SEW FRONT TO BACK

1. With right sides together, matching seams, pin one side of the dress back to the dress front at the shoulder seams.

2. Begin at the end of the sleeve and sew, following the seam line to the little dot.

43

Dollhouse People

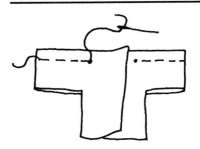

3. Repeat for the other side.

4. Press seams open.

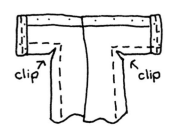

3. Repeat for other side.

4. Clip as shown.

clip   clip

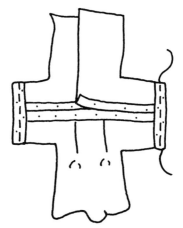

TO HEM SLEEVES

1. Turn under the sleeve bottoms ¼ inch (¾ cm). Press.

2. Hem, using the running stitch.

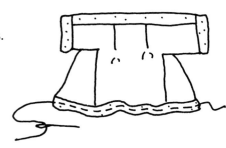

FINALLY

1. Turn under the dress bottom ¼ inch (¾ cm). Press.

2. Hem, using the running stitch.

TO SEW SIDE SEAMS

1. With right sides together, matching seams, pin the front of the dress to the back.

2. Begin at the sleeve bottom and sew, following the sleeve seam. Turn the corner and continue, following the side seam to the bottom of the dress.

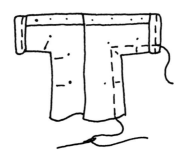

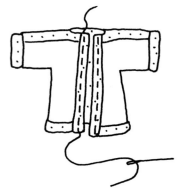

3. Turn under the center back of the dress ¼ inch (¾ cm). Press.

4. Hem, using the running stitch.

Elizabeth & Jonathan

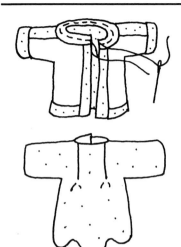

5. Turn under the neck of the dress ¼ inch (¾ cm). Press.

6. Hem, using the running stitch.

7. Turn the dress right side out.

Here are some ways to keep the dress closed:

Sew a snap or hook to the back of the dress.

Sew a narrow ribbon to the neck of the dress and tie a bow.

Place a ribbon around the waist and tie a bow.

TO MAKE ELIZABETH'S DRESS SPECIAL

1. Add lace or trimming to the sleeves. This is easier to do before you have put the dress together. Follow the instructions until you get to "To Sew Side Seams."

Now follow these instructions:

a. Cut the trimming to fit the sleeve bottoms.

b. Pin the trimming to the right side of the hemmed sleeves.

c. Sew the trimming in place, using the running stitch.

d. Continue with "To Sew Side Seams."

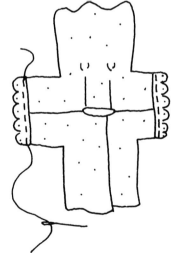

2. Sew lace trimming or ribbon around the neck or hem of the dress.

3. Sew tiny beads to the front and back of the dress for buttons.

45

Dollhouse People

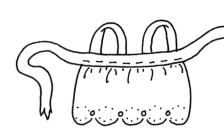

Elizabeth's Pinafore

Elizabeth's pinafore is made from a gathered piece of lace sewn to a length of ribbon.

wrong side

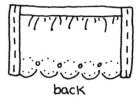

back

right side

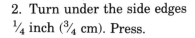

front

PINAFORE

1. Cut a piece of gathered 1-inch-wide (2½-cm-wide) lace gathered 3½ inches (9 cm) long. If your lace is not already gathered, cut a piece of lace 5 inches (12½ cm) long and gather it to equal 3½ inches (9 cm).

2. Turn under the side edges ¼ inch (¾ cm). Press.

3. Hem the side edges, using the running stitch.

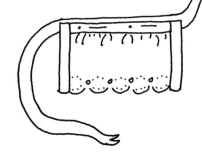

WAISTBAND

1. Cut a piece of narrow ribbon 10 inches (25 cm) long. If your ribbon is too wide, you can fold it in half, lengthwise, and press.

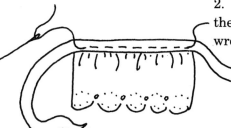

2. Center the gathered edge of the right side of the lace to the wrong side of the ribbon. Pin.

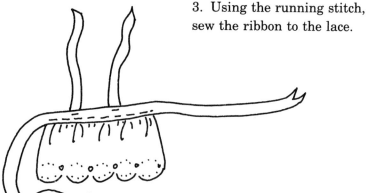

3. Using the running stitch, sew the ribbon to the lace.

STRAPS

1. Cut two pieces of ribbon 2 inches (5 cm) long.

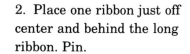

2. Place one ribbon just off center and behind the long ribbon. Pin.

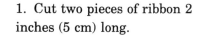

3. Sew the ribbon in place.

Elizabeth & Jonathan

4. Repeat for the other side.

5. Place the opposite end of the ribbon behind the long ribbon close to the edge of the lace. Pin.

6. Repeat for the other side.

FINALLY

1. Fit the pinafore to Elizabeth. Adjust the straps if needed.

2. Sew the straps to the ribbon.

3. Put the pinafore on Elizabeth and tie it with a bow.

TO MAKE YOUR PINAFORE SPECIAL

1. Use narrow lace for the straps.

2. Use a pretty fabric for the pinafore, instead of lace.

3. Add a pocket, or two.

Dollhouse People

Jonathan's Clothing

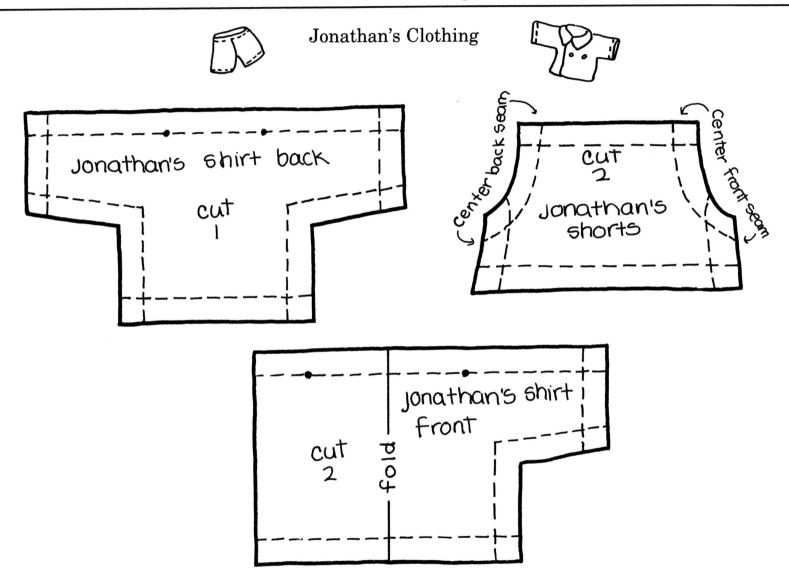

Jonathan's shirt back

cut 1

Center back seam

Center front seam

cut 2

Jonathan's shorts

Jonathan's shirt front

cut 2

fold

Elizabeth & Jonathan

SUPPLIES

Basic supplies *(introductory chapter)*

White cotton fabric *(for shirt)*

Cotton fabric *(for shorts)*

Narrow ribbon *(for straps)*

Tiny beads or buttons *(for shirt)*

Jonathan's Pants

Jonathan's pants are like his father's, only smaller. Using the pattern for Jonathan's pants, follow the instructions for Charles's pants.

Using the pattern for Jonathan's shirt, follow the instructions for Charles's shirt.

When you are ready to sew on the buttons, place them as shown here.

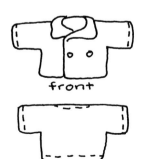

front

back

Jonathan's Shirt

Except for the placement of the buttons, Jonathan's shirt is like his father's.

CHAPTER FIVE

New Arrivals:

Baby, Mr. Buff, Bumkins

It wasn't long before the Littlefields filled every room! Charles finished wallpapering the nursery just in time for the arrival of the new baby.

Elizabeth and Jonathan brought their new sister wonderful presents. They brought her a cat Lizzie found under the porch and a dog that happened to follow Jonathan home.

Elizabeth named the cat Bumkins. Jonathan called the dog Mr. Buff. The parents named the baby after Sarah's mother, Lucy.

THE BABY

SUPPLIES

Doll Body Supplies *(Chapter Two)*

The baby is a tiny simplified version of the rest of the family. Once you've made one, you will want to make twins . . . triplets . . . !

3 inches (7½ cm) of gathered lace *(1 to 3 inches wide [2½ to 7½ cm wide])*

12 inches (30 cm) of narrow ribbon

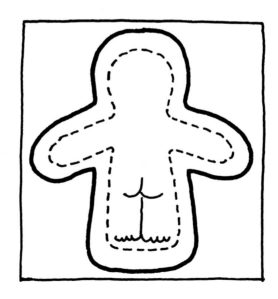

New Arrivals

CUTTING OUT THE PATTERN

Cut two squares of cotton muslin, the same size as the squares around the patterns. Trace the pattern.

TO SEW THE BABY

1. With right sides together, match the front of the baby to the back. Pin the squares together.

2. Begin at the bottom edge of the baby and sew, following the seam line around the baby. Finish at the opposite bottom edge, leaving the bottom open for stuffing.

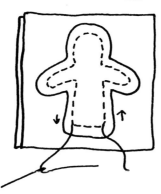

TO CUT

1. Following the cutting line, cut around the baby.

2. Clip as shown, under the arms. Be careful not to clip into your seams!

3. Carefully turn the baby right side out as you did for the rest of the family.

TO STUFF

1. Stuff the baby with fiberfill, as you did in Chapter Two.

2. Turn under the bottom edge of the baby $\frac{1}{4}$ inch ($\frac{3}{4}$ cm). Pin the bottom edge closed.

3. Sew the bottom closed using the overcasting stitch.

BABY HAIR

Sew a tiny bit of yarn or embroidery thread to the top of the baby's head. Not too much! Babies don't have very much hair.

FINALLY

To make a happy healthy baby, color the cheeks, chin, belly, knees, and bottom with a pink-colored pencil or crayon.

53

Dollhouse People

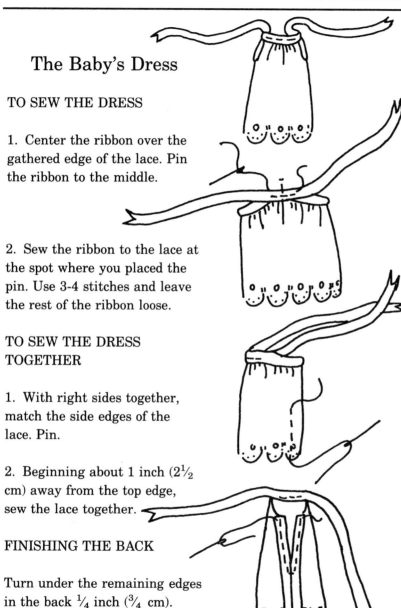

The Baby's Dress

TO SEW THE DRESS

1. Center the ribbon over the gathered edge of the lace. Pin the ribbon to the middle.

2. Sew the ribbon to the lace at the spot where you placed the pin. Use 3-4 stitches and leave the rest of the ribbon loose.

TO SEW THE DRESS TOGETHER

1. With right sides together, match the side edges of the lace. Pin.

2. Beginning about 1 inch (2½ cm) away from the top edge, sew the lace together.

FINISHING THE BACK

Turn under the remaining edges in the back ¼ inch (¾ cm). Hem using the running stitch.

FINALLY

Sew one upper corner of the back of the lace dress to the ribbon. This will leave a tiny opening for the baby's arm. Repeat for other side.

Mr. Buff and Bumkins

SUPPLIES

Doll Body Supplies (*Chapter Two*)

Pipe cleaner

The dog and cat are similar to the baby, but they have tails! The tails are stuffed with a pipe cleaner. You can bend the tails to help make the animals stand!

First, read about the tail. Then, using the animal patterns, follow the instructions for making the baby.

New Arrivals

THE TAIL

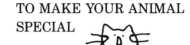

When you sew around
your animal, continue sewing
around the tail, but remember
to leave the bottom of the body
open for stuffing. Clip the tail
as shown, and the ears too
when you are making the cat.

Instead of stuffing the tail,
cut a piece of pipe cleaner as
long as the tail and body of the
animal. Insert the pipe cleaner
into the tail and sew the body
closed, hiding the pipe cleaner.

TO MAKE YOUR ANIMAL SPECIAL

TO COLOR

Use your imagination! Color
your pet with paints, colored
pencils, crayons, or pens. They
don't have to look like the ones
in the book. How about a
spotted cat and a striped dog?

WHISKERS

For an extra special cat, give
him whiskers.

Using heavy thread, like
embroidery thread, insert the
needle with the thread in one
side of the cat's face and out
the other. (Don't worry, he
won't feel a thing!) Clip the
whiskers. If you are using
embroidery thread, separate
the strands of thread. Put a
tiny dab of clear nail polish or
glue where the whiskers come
out of the cat's face. This will
make the whiskers stand out,
and he won't lose them.

CHAPTER SIX

Grandmother & Grandfather

The house was in a scurry of activity. Grandmother and Grandfather Littlefield were coming for Christmas!

There was so much to do! Sarah and Charles went to the kitchen to plan the holiday menu, and the children went upstairs to clean their rooms.

But, before anyone was quite ready, there was a knock at the door.

Dollhouse People

Grandmother's Clothing

SUPPLIES

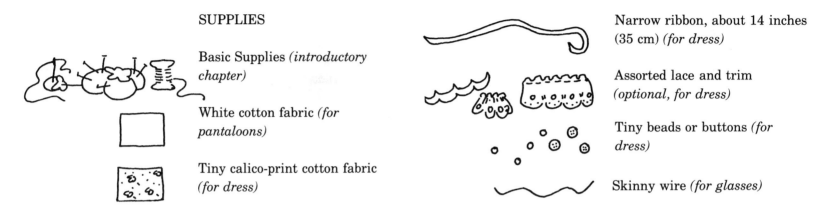

Basic Supplies *(introductory chapter)*

White cotton fabric *(for pantaloons)*

Tiny calico-print cotton fabric *(for dress)*

Narrow ribbon, about 14 inches (35 cm) *(for dress)*

Assorted lace and trim *(optional, for dress)*

Tiny beads or buttons *(for dress)*

Skinny wire *(for glasses)*

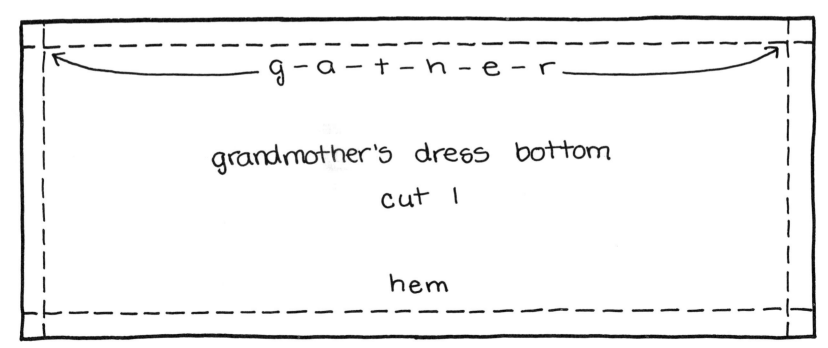

g-a-t-h-e-r

grandmother's dress bottom

cut 1

hem

Grandmother & Grandfather

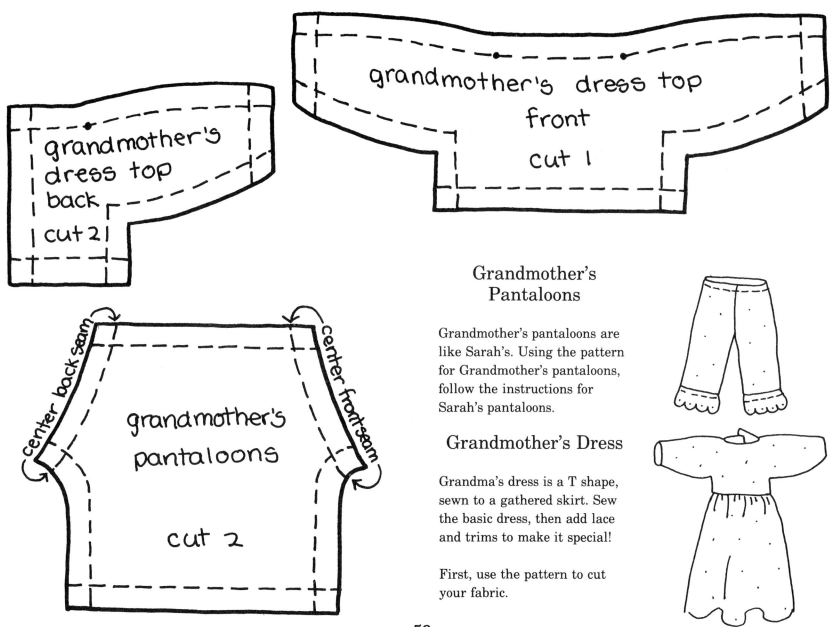

grandmother's dress top back

cut 2

grandmother's dress top front

cut 1

center back seam

center front seam

grandmother's pantaloons

cut 2

Grandmother's Pantaloons

Grandmother's pantaloons are like Sarah's. Using the pattern for Grandmother's pantaloons, follow the instructions for Sarah's pantaloons.

Grandmother's Dress

Grandma's dress is a T shape, sewn to a gathered skirt. Sew the basic dress, then add lace and trims to make it special!

First, use the pattern to cut your fabric.

Dollhouse People

DRESS TOP

1. With right sides together, match seams of one side of the top front of the dress to the top of the back. Pin.

2. Begin at the end of the sleeve, sew across the top, following the seam line to the dot.

3. Repeat for other side.

4. Press the seams open.

5. Turn under the sleeve bottoms ¼ inch (¾ cm). Press.

6. Hem using the running stitch.

TO SEW SIDE SEAMS

1. With right sides together, match the side and sleeve seams. Pin the front of the dress top to the back.

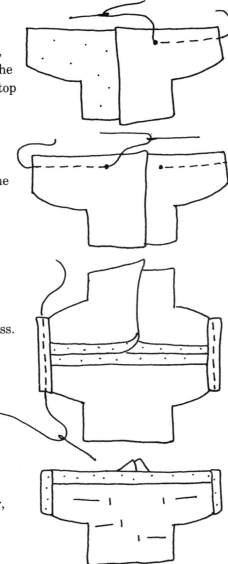

2. Begin at the edge of the sleeve and sew, following the seam line along the edge of the sleeve. Turn the corner and continue down the side to the bottom edge of the dress top.

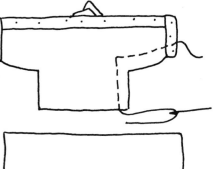

DRESS SKIRT

1. Turn under the bottom edge of the skirt ¼ inch (¾ cm). Press.

2. Hem using the running stitch.

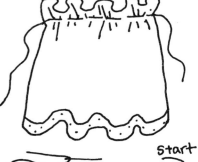

3. Gather the top of the skirt to 5¼ inches (13 cm), as explained in Chapter One.

4. With right sides together, match the gathered edge of the skirt to the bottom edge of the dress top. Pin the top and the skirt together. Make sure your gathering is even.

5. Begin at one side of the dress and sew.

Start

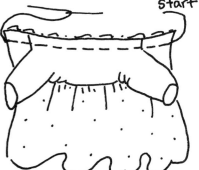

Grandmother & Grandfather

TO FINISH SEWING DRESS TOGETHER

1. With right sides together, match center back seams of the dress skirt. Pin.

2. Begin at the bottom edge of the skirt and sew, following the seam line to the dot.

FINALLY

1. Turn under the remaining center back seam $\frac{1}{4}$ inch ($\frac{3}{4}$ cm) on each side. Press.

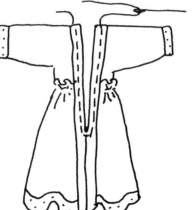

2. Begin at the dot. Hem one side using the running stitch, finishing at the neck.

3. Repeat for other side.

4. Turn under the neck seam $\frac{1}{4}$ inch ($\frac{3}{4}$ cm). Press.

5. Hem using the running stitch.

6. Turn the dress right side out.

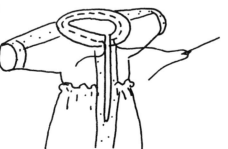

7. To keep the dress closed, attach the narrow ribbon to the waist and tie a bow. If your ribbon looks too wide, fold it in half and press it.

TO MAKE YOUR DRESS SPECIAL

1. Add lace or trim.

2. Add tiny beads for buttons.

3. Add a ruffle (*see Sarah's skirt*).

Dollhouse People

Grandmother's Shawl

Grandmother's shawl is simple to make.

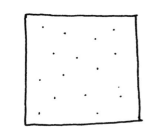

1. Cut a 6-inch (15-cm) square out of cotton fabric.

2. Fold the square into a triangle.

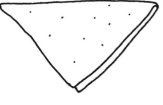

TO MAKE YOUR SHAWL SPECIAL

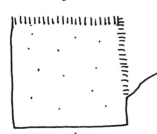

1. Fray the edges. Just pull the threads along the edges of the shawl.

2. Look for fabrics with different patterns and textures. Plaids are pretty. Wools are warm. A sock is nice and soft.

(But, before you cut one up make sure the foot that wears it will not be needing it!)

nice socks!

Grandmother's Glasses

Glasses are easy to make. You can use these instructions to make glasses for the entire family.

Use a piece of skinny wire. Brass is nice, but anything skinny and easy to bend is fine.

1. Cut a piece of wire about 4 inches (10 cm) long.

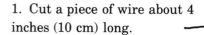

2. Make a little loop about 1½ inches (4 cm) from one end of the wire.

3. Make another little loop right after the first loop.

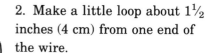

4. Bend the straight ends to fit the head.

5. Fit the glasses to the doll, tucking the ends into the doll's hair. Cut the ends if they are too long.

Grandmother & Grandfather

Grandfather's Clothes

SUPPLIES

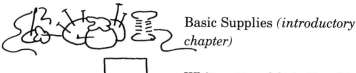

Basic Supplies *(introductory chapter)*

White cotton fabric *(for shirt)*

Cotton fabric *(for pants)*

Narrow ribbon *(for suspenders)*

Tiny beads or buttons *(for shirt and vest)*

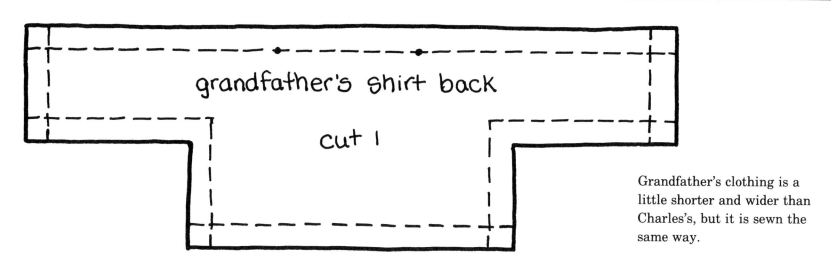

grandfather's shirt back

cut 1

Grandfather's clothing is a little shorter and wider than Charles's, but it is sewn the same way.

Grandfather's Shirt

Using the pattern for Grandfather's shirt, follow the instructions for Charles's shirt.

Grandfather's Pants

Using the pattern for Grandfather's pants, follow the instructions for Charles's pants.

Dollhouse People

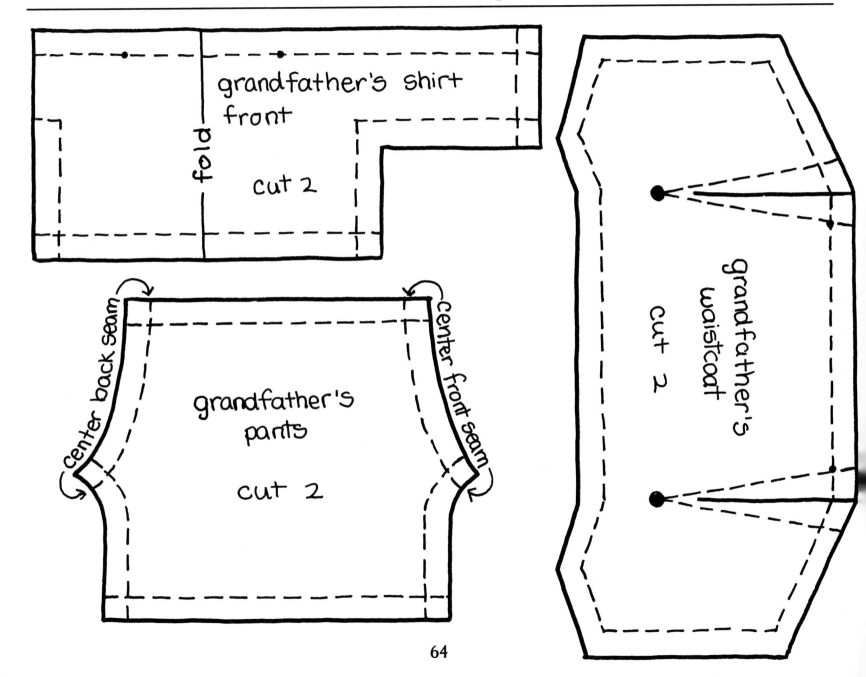

grandfather's shirt
front

fold

cut 2

center back seam

center front seam

grandfather's
pants

cut 2

grandfather's
waistcoat

cut 2

Grandmother & Grandfather

Grandfather's Waistcoat

Use the waistcoat pattern to cut your fabric, as explained in Chapter One. Remember you are cutting two pieces, one for the outside and one for the lining.

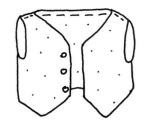

TO CUT ARMHOLES

1. With right sides together, matching seams, pin the two pattern pieces together.

2. Cut through both layers of fabric, following the cutting lines from the top edge of the waistcoat to the big dots.

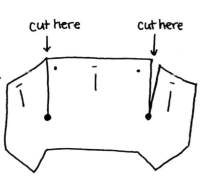

TO SEW

1. Beginning at the little dot, sew, following the seam line down one side of your armhole cut, and back up the other. Continue sewing around, following the seam line to the other armhole cut. Continue along the opposite armhole and back up to the other dot. Leave the opening between the two little dots unsewn, so you can turn the waistcoat right side out.

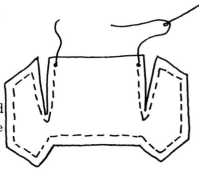

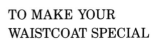

2. Turn the waistcoats right side out. Press.

3. Turn under both top edges $\frac{1}{4}$ inch ($\frac{3}{4}$ cm), so that no raw edges are seen. Press.

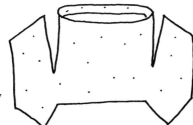

TO FINISH ARMHOLES

1. Tuck the top point of the front of the waistcoats $\frac{1}{4}$ inch ($\frac{3}{4}$ cm) into the top of the back opening. Pin.

2. Sew in place.

3. Repeat for other side.

FINALLY

Sew the remaining opening closed using the running stitch.

TO MAKE YOUR WAISTCOAT SPECIAL

1. Use a different color or pattern for the lining.

2. Sew or glue on tiny beads or buttons.

CHAPTER SEVEN

Goodnight! Goodnight!

The entire family was busy preparing for the holidays. There were presents to wrap and goodies to bake, with the children's help, of course.

By Christmas Eve almost everyone was exhausted. Grandmother and Grandfather tried to put the children to bed by reading them a special story. But Grandfather fell fast asleep first!

Dollhouse People

Nightgowns and Nightshirts

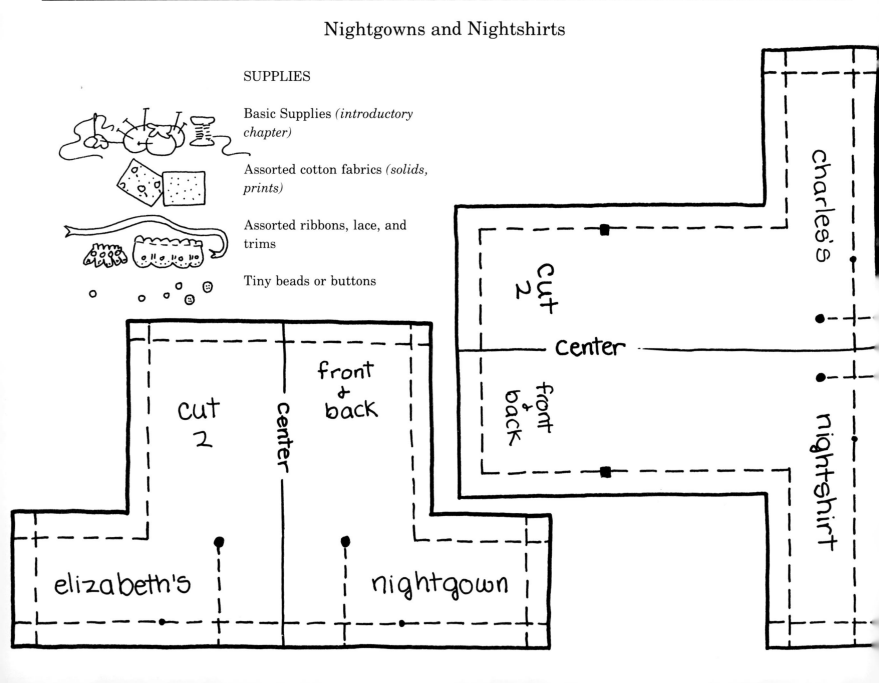

SUPPLIES

Basic Supplies *(introductory chapter)*

Assorted cotton fabrics *(solids, prints)*

Assorted ribbons, lace, and trims

Tiny beads or buttons

cut 2

center

front & back

charles's nightshirt

cut 2

center

front & back

elizabeth's

nightgown

Goodnight! Goodnight!

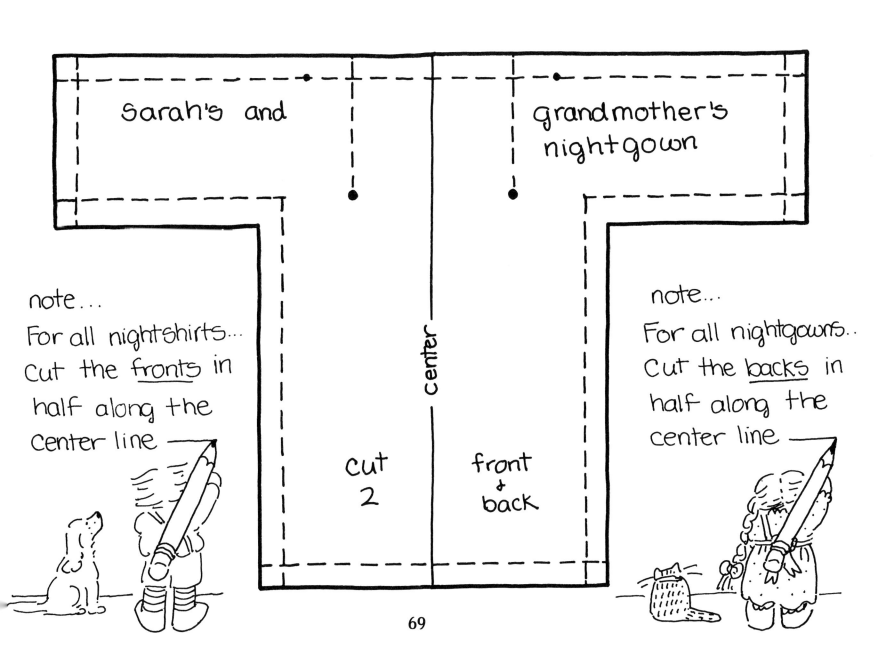

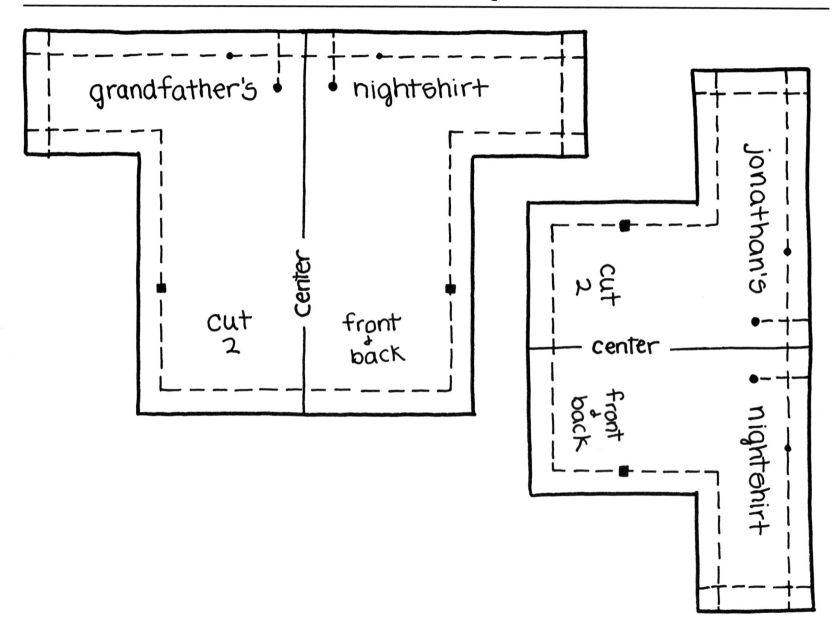

grandfather's nightshirt

Center

cut 2

front & back

jonathan's nightshirt

cut 2

center

front & back

Goodnight! Goodnight!

Sarah's Nightgown

Sarah's nightgown is like Elizabeth's dress with gathered sleeves to give it fullness. Start with the basic nightgown, then add lace and ribbons to make your nightgown special. The possibilities seem endless. You can even use this pattern to make a dress.

Using the pattern for Sarah's nightgown, follow the instructions for Elizabeth's dress. Finally, when you think you are finished, it is time to gather the sleeve bottoms.

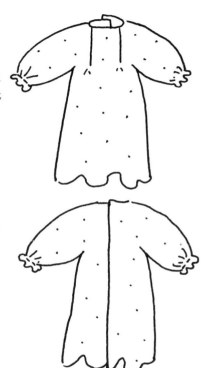

TO GATHER SLEEVE BOTTOMS

1. Without knotting your thread and leaving at least 3 inches (8 cm) of excess thread, sew around the bottom of the sleeve, ¼ inch (¾ cm) from the edge, using the running stitch. Stop when you return to where you began, and again leave at least 3 inches (8 cm) of thread hanging.

2. Repeat for other sleeve.

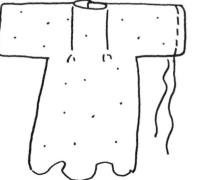
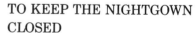

3. With threads hanging, put the nightgown on your doll.

4. Push one sleeve up along the arm of the doll.

5. Pull your threads together, gathering the sleeve to fit your dolls arm. Not too tight! Secure by tying the threads into a double knot. Cut the excess thread.

6. Repeat for other sleeve.

TO KEEP THE NIGHTGOWN CLOSED

1. Sew a snap or hook to the back of the nightgown.

2. Sew a narrow ribbon to the neck of the nightgown and tie a bow.

3. Place a ribbon around the waist and tie a bow.

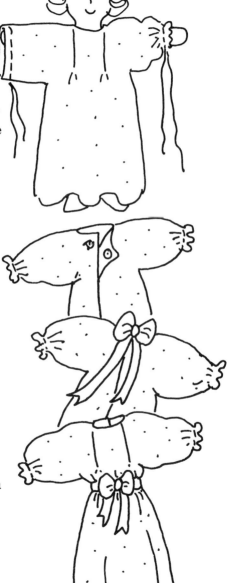

Dollhouse People

TO MAKE YOUR NIGHTGOWN SPECIAL

1. Make a ruffled collar.

a. Cut a piece of lace about 7 inches (18 cm) long.

b. Using the running stitch, gather the lace to fit the neck of the nightgown.

c. Pin the ruffle to the inside of the neck of the nightgown.

d. Sew the ruffle to the neck of the nightgown.

2. Sew lace or ribbon to the sleeves of the nightgown or to the bottom edge.

3. Make a nightgown out of plain white cotton, then add lots of lace and ribbons.

Grandmother's Nightgown

Grandmother's nightgown is like Sarah's, only shorter. Use the pattern and instructions for Sarah's nightgown, but make it ¼ inch (¾ cm) shorter than Sarah's.

Elizabeth's Nightgown

Elizabeth's nightgown is also like her mother's, only smaller.
Using the pattern for Elizabeth's nightgown, follow the instructions for Sarah's nightgown.

Charles's Nightshirt

Charles's nightshirt is similar to the nightgown, but it is worn backward. It has a small tuck in the back and an opening in the front. The shirt also has slits on the sides because it is not as full.
Using the pattern for Charles's nightshirt, follow the instructions for Elizabeth's dress. Remember, the front will be the back and the back the front.

TO MAKE THE SLITS

When sewing the side seams, sew only to the square, instead of to the bottom of the nightshirt. Turn under the

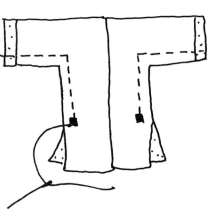

Goodnight! Goodnight!

remaining edges of the sides of the nightshirt ¼ inch (¾ cm) and hem using the running stitch. Follow Elizabeth's instructions to hem the rest of the nightshirt.

TO MAKE YOUR NIGHTSHIRT SPECIAL

1. Sew or glue buttons or beads to the front panel of the nightshirt.

2. Add a pocket (see "Charles's Shirt").

3. Make a night cap!

Grandfather's Nightshirt

Grandfather's nightshirt is like Charles's only shorter and wider!

Using the pattern for Grandfather's nightshirt, follow the instructions for Charles's nightshirt.

Jonathan's Nightshirt

Jonathan's nightshirt is a tiny copy of his father's.

Using the pattern for Jonathan's nightshirt, follow the instructions for Charles's nightshirt.

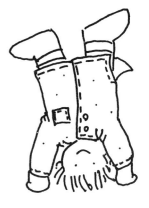

Goodnight Bears

Use these little patterns to make tiny stuffed bears for the children. Just trace the patterns onto paper and cut the bears out of felt. Sew around the bears using the overcasting stitch; before you sew all the way around put in a little stuffing. Stitch little eyes and noses out of colored thread.

papa

cut 2

mama

cut 2

Bedtime Story

Make a tiny book! Take three or four small pieces of paper, fold them in half, then sew them together along the fold. Write a tiny story and draw tiny pictures. You can make lots of books—all shapes and sizes.

baby

cut 2

Merry Christmas!

On Christmas morning the children rushed downstairs! When they reached the living room they could hardly believe their eyes. There was Santa munching on the cookies they had baked.

The children introduced Santa to the rest of the family, except Grandfather. They couldn't find him anywhere!

Santa told the children not to worry, he and Grandfather had already met. Who do *you* think Santa really was?